We Love DADDY

BY
RUPERT FAWCETT

BXTREE

First published in 1997 by Boxtree, an imprint of Macmillan Publishers Ltd,
25 Eccleston Place, London, SW1W 9NF and Basingstoke

Associated companies throughout the world

ISBN: 0 7522 2244 9

Copyright © 1997 Rupert Fawcett

10 9 8 7 6 5 4 3 2

Printed and bound in Great Britain by Redwood Books, Trowbridge, Wiltshire.

A CIP catalogue entry for this book is available from the British Library

Not being content with the huge success of his cartoon character, Fred, whose greeting cards continue to sell in millions, Rupert Fawcett has come up with another brilliant creation in DADDY.

WE LOVE DADDY, the second book in the DADDY series, contains 60 cartoons following the trials and tribulations of the hapless DADDY as he struggles to come to terms with the realities of parenthood.

Rupert was born and brought up in West London where he still lives with his wife and (surprise, surprise) two small children.

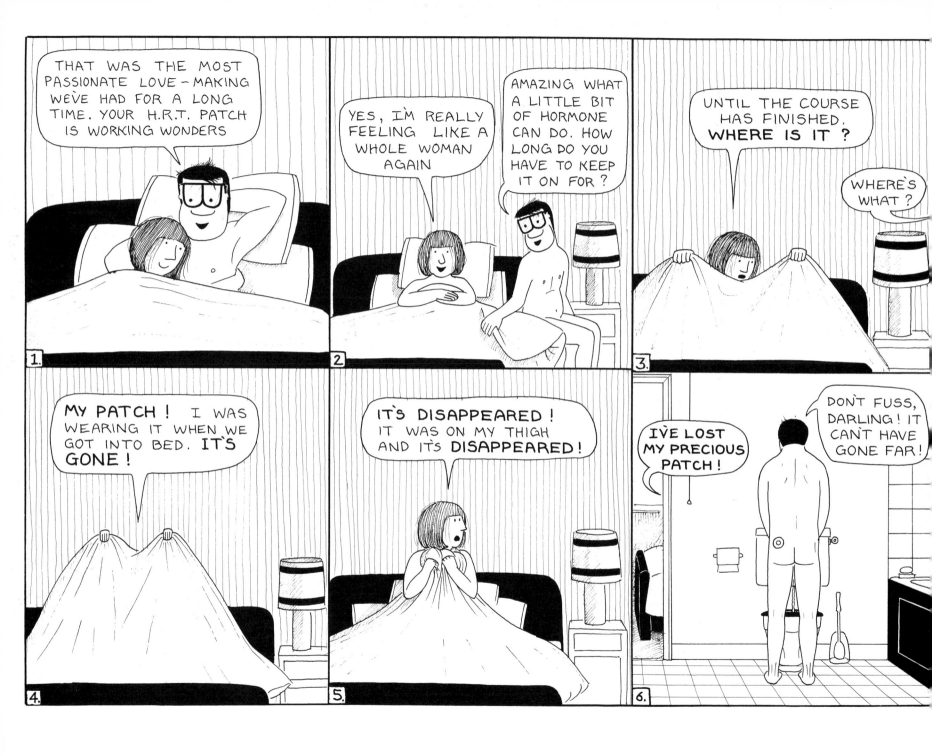

1. HI, GUYS. WELCOME TO ANOTHER MEETING OF THE FATHERS' SUPPORT GROUP

2. LAST WEEK STEPHEN SHARED A PERSONAL PROBLEM WITH US AND NOW DANIEL WOULD LIKE TO RESPOND ON BEHALF OF THE GROUP.

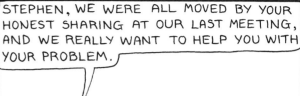

3. STEPHEN, WE WERE ALL MOVED BY YOUR HONEST SHARING AT OUR LAST MEETING, AND WE REALLY WANT TO HELP YOU WITH YOUR PROBLEM.

4. WE HAVE COME UP WITH AN 'AFFIRMATION' WHICH WE FEEL COULD SHIFT YOUR MENTAL ATTITUDE TO THE PROBLEM, AND IMPROVE YOUR SELF-ESTEEM.

5. WE WOULD LIKE YOU TO REPEAT IT ONE HUNDRED TIMES, EVERY MORNING AND EVERY NIGHT. O.K. GUYS ?.....

6. I'VE GOT A BALD PATCH BUT I'M STILL A LOVEABLE HUMAN BEING! I'VE GOT A BALD PATCH BUT I'M STILL A LOVEABLE HUMAN BEING!

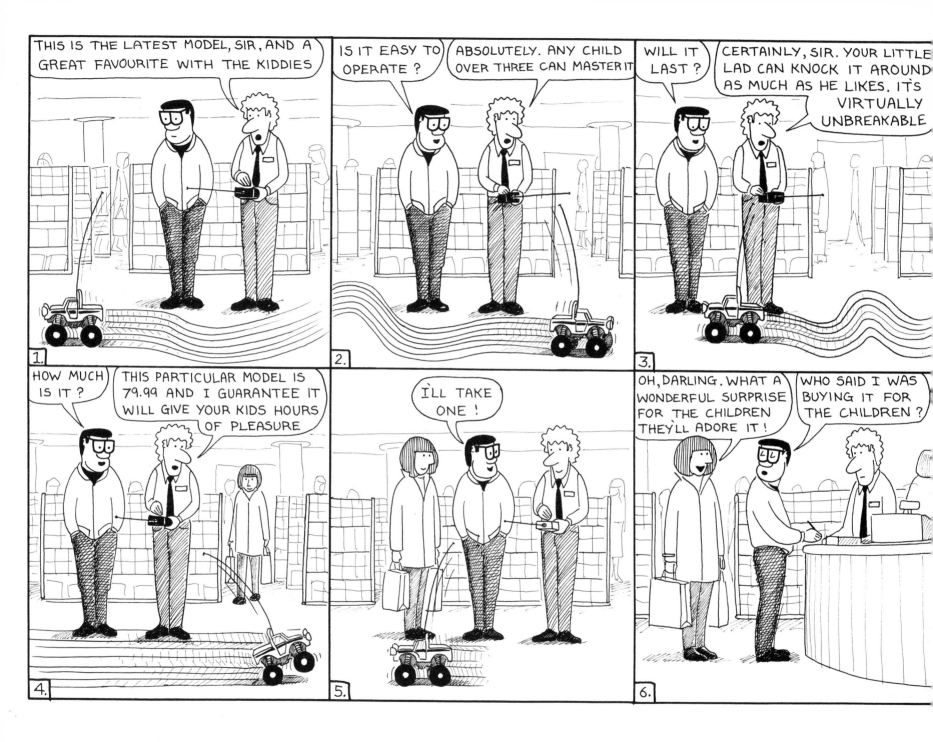

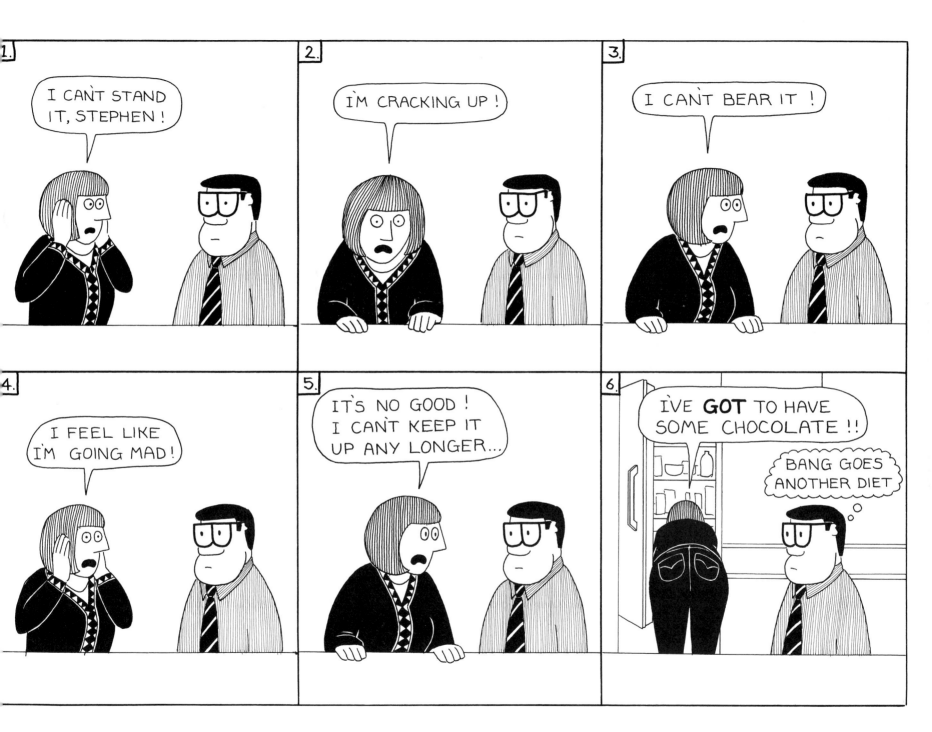

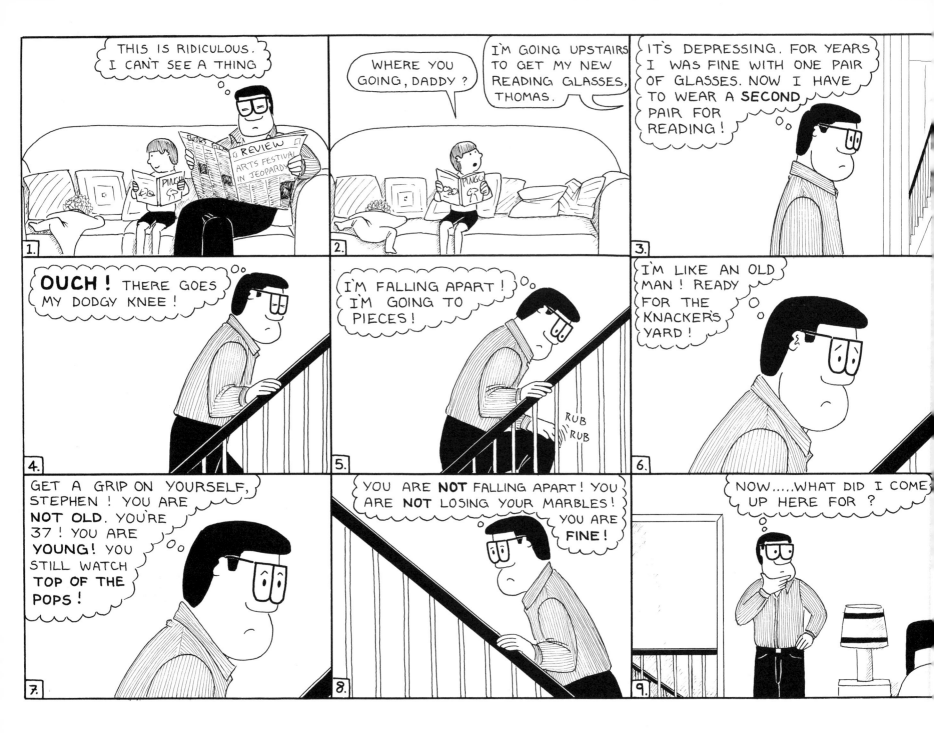